Stories
of
GREAT PEOPLE

Leonardo's palette

Gerry Bailey and Karen Foster

Illustrated by Leighton Noyes
and Karen Radford

🌱 Crabtree Publishing Company

www.crabtreebooks.com

MR. RUMMAGE has a stall piled high with interesting objects—and he has a great story to tell about each and every one of his treasures.

DIGBY PLATT is an antique collector. Every Saturday he picks up a bargain at Mr. Rummage's antique stall and loves listening to the story behind his new 'find'.

HANNAH PLATT is Digby's argumentative, older sister—and she doesn't believe a word that Mr. Rummage says!

PIXIE the market's fortuneteller sells incense, lotions and potions, candles, mandalas, and crystals inside her exotic stall.

YOUSSEF has traveled to many places around the world. He carries a bag full of souvenirs from his exciting journeys.

Mr. POLLOCK's toy stall is filled with string puppets, rocking horses, model planes, wooden animals—and he makes them all himself!

Crabtree Publishing Company
www.crabtreebooks.com

Other books in the series

Cleopatra's coin

Columbus's chart

Martin Luther King, Jr.'s microphone

Armstrong's moon rock

The Wright Brothers' glider

Shakespeare's quill

Marco Polo's silk purse

Mother Teresa's alms bowl

Sitting Bull's tomahawk

Library and Archives Canada Cataloguing in Publication

Bailey, Gerry
        Leonardo's pallete / Gerry Bailey and Karen Foster ; illustrated by Leighton Noyes and Karen Radford.

(Stories of great people)
Includes index.
ISBN 978-0-7787-3687-5 (bound).--ISBN 978-0-7787-3709-4 (pbk.)

        1. Leonardo, da Vinci, 1452-1519--Juvenile fiction. 2. Painters--Italy--Biography--Juvenile fiction. 3. Scientists--Italy--Biography--Juvenile fiction. I. Radford, Karen II. Noyes, Leighton III. Foster, Karen, 1959- IV. Title. V. Series.

PZ7.B15Le 2008   j823'.92   C2007-907623-8

Library of Congress Cataloging-in-Publication Data

Bailey, Gerry.
 Leonardo's palette / Gerry Bailey and Karen Foster ; illustrated by Leighton Noyes and Karen Radford.
      p. cm.
 Includes bibliographical references and index.
 ISBN-13: 978-0-7787-3687-5 (rlb)
 ISBN-10: 0-7787-3687-3 (rlb)
 ISBN-13: 978-0-7787-3709-4 (pb)
 ISBN-10: 0-7787-3709-8 (pb)
 1. Leonardo, da Vinci, 1452-1519--Juvenile literature. 2. Artists--Italy--Biography--Juvenile literature. I. Foster, Karen, 1964- II. Noyes, Leighton. III. Radford, Karen. IV. Title.
 N6923.L33B35 2008
 709.2--dc22
 [B]
                                            2007051258

Crabtree Publishing Company
www.crabtreebooks.com   1-800-387-7650

Published in Canada
Crabtree Publishing
616 Welland Ave.
St. Catharines, Ontario
L2M 5V6

Published in the United States
Crabtree Publishing
PMB16A
350 Fifth Ave., Suite 3308
New York, NY 10118

Published by CRABTREE PUBLISHING COMPANY
Copyright © **2008** Diverta Ltd.

Leonardo's Palette

Table of Contents

Every Saturday morning, Knicknack Market comes to life. The street vendors are there almost before the sun is up. And by the time you and I are out of bed, the stalls are built, the boxes are opened, and all the goods are carefully laid out on display.

Objects are piled high. Some are laid out on velvet: precious necklaces and jeweled swords. Others  stand upright at the back: large, framed pictures of very important people, lamps made from tasseled satin, and old-fashioned cash registers— the kind that jingle when the drawers are opened. And then there are things that stay in their boxes all day, waiting for the right customer to come along: war medals laid out in straight lines, watches on leather straps, and utensils in polished silver for all those special occasions.

But Mr. Rummage's stall is different. Mr. Rummage of Knicknack Market has a stall piled high with a disorderly jumble of things that no one could ever want.

Who needs a stuffed mouse? Or a broken umbrella? Or a pair of false teeth?

Mr. Rummage has them all. And, as you can imagine, they don't cost a lot!

Rummage's
Antiques

Digby Platt—10-year-old collector of antiques—was on his way to see his friend Mr. Rummage of Knicknack Market. It was Saturday and, as usual, his allowance money was burning a hole in his pocket. But Digby wasn't going to spend it on any old thing. Oh no, it had to be something rare and interesting for his collection, something from Mr. Rummage's incredible stall.

Hannah, his older sister, was with him. Digby didn't see why she always had to tag along. What he didn't know was that Hannah had secret doubts about the value of Mr. Rummage's treasures. She felt, for some big-sisterly reason, that she had to stop her little brother from buying yet another useless piece of junk.

"Good morning, good morning," said Mr. Rummage, as Digby began the usual Saturday search through his friend's treasures.

"Good morning, Mr. Rummage," said Digby cheerfully as he dug his hands into a soft pile of felt hats. His thumb stuck through the hole of something hard and flat. Digby hooked his thumb around the object and drew it out from under the heap of hats.

"Wow, what's this?" he asked.

"Hi Mr. Rummage," said Hannah. Then she turned to Digby, "Why do you always ask dumb questions, Digby? Can't you see it's a **palette**?"

"A what?"

"A painter's palette," sighed Hannah, "the thing they mix their paints on before they put them on the canvas. Everyone knows that."

"Really?" said Digby as he picked up an artist's hat from the pile and placed it on his head. "Look, now I'm a painter!"

Hannah snickered as the beret slid over Digby's ears.

"I have to admit it, you look the part," said Mr. Rummage, "just like Leonardo himself. In fact, believe it or not, that was one of the great Leonardo da Vinci's favorite palettes."

"Oh no, here we go again!" groaned Hannah dramatically.

Leonardo da Vinci

Leonardo da Vinci was born on Saturday April 15, 1452 at "three o'clock of the night." We know this because Leonardo's grandfather made a note of it. His birthplace was probably the Italian village of Anchiano near Vinci and Florence. (Da Vinci means "from Vinci.")

Leonardo's family

Leonardo's father, Ser Piero, was an important local official, while his mother was a peasant girl called Caterina. Leonardo's father never married her, so the boy was **illegitimate**. A year after his son's birth, Ser Piero married a woman from a wealthy family. Poor Caterina, on the other hand, was married off to a cow herder. At first, Leonardo lived with his grandparents in the country, but soon he came to live with his father, Ser Piero, and his wife. Both Caterina and Ser Piero each had more children and eventually supplied Leonardo with 17 half sisters and brothers!

Let's find out more...

Brilliant apprentice

At the age of 14, Leonardo became an apprentice in the workshop of Andrea del Verrocchio, an important Florentine artist. Leonardo worked alongside other famous artists of the day, such as Botticelli and Perugino, and like them began his apprenticeship by mixing colors, sanding down wooden panels, modeling in clay, preparing backgrounds, and painting simple parts of pictures. He probably also sketched artist's models or dressed them for a painting or sculpture.

ON AUGUST 5, 1473 LEONARDO MADE A PEN AND INK DRAWING OF THE ARNO VALLEY. IT'S HIS FIRST KNOWN AND DATED WORK. HE DREW IT IN A WAY THAT MADE IT LOOK REAL. NO ONE HAD WORKED IN THIS STYLE BEFORE.

LEONARDO'S EXTRAORDINARY TALENT AMAZED HIS FATHER AND HIS TEACHER.

New perspective

Leonardo probably found the day-to-day tasks at the workshop easy. He needed more challenges, so he put his mind to learning geometry, math, and perspective. He quickly became an expert in all of these subjects and he was better than anyone else at making his pictures look real. He also taught himself to paint in oils—the latest craze.

"**W**as this his very first palette?" asked Hannah, mischievously.

"Well, no," said Mr. Rummage, "but I'm glad you asked, because, just like a certain young lady I know, Leonardo was a curious child who had many interests. But as he grew up, he drove his teachers crazy with all his questions."

"Oh," said Hannah, as her cheeks grew.

"Anyway," continued Mr. Rummage, winking at Digby, "when Leonardo was 14, his father took some of his drawings to show his close friend, the famous Florentine painter Andrea del Verrocchio. Ser Piero wanted to know whether his son had any talent."

"But if he was a friend, he wouldn't want to say that Leonardo's stuff was no good, would he?" asked Digby.

"Well, he didn't need to pretend," said Mr. Rummage. "Verrocchio was amazed by his skills and took him on as his assistant."

"Leonardo must have been really good," said Digby.

"Too good," said Mr. Rummage. "When Verrocchio gave him the job of painting an angel in his *Baptism of Christ* picture, Leonardo did so much better than his master, that Verrocchio decided never to paint again."

"Sounds a little extreme," laughed Hannah, beginning to enjoy the story.

"Leonardo loved nature and enjoyed studying things around him," said Mr. Rummage. He was also a **geologist** and **paleontologist**."

"A paleo-what?' asked Digby.

"He studied rocks and stuff like that," explained Hannah.

"At that time," said Mr. Rummage, "most paintings had a landscape in the background. They were usually make-believe, fantasy scenes. But Leonardo's were different. He made them look real and dramatic. He drew detail right down to the sunlight on leaves."

Just then, Pixie the market's fortuneteller wandered past, holding a bag of fossils and polished stones.

"Leonardo knew a lot about the rocks and fossils in the area where he grew up. He could draw the tiniest veins on a pebble and put a sparkle on·water," she said.

"Wow!" exclaimed Digby.

"He even experimented with pieces of colored glass—looking through them to see how they changed the colors of nature," Pixie went on.

"I see what you mean," said Hannah. "Everything looks different through my cool tinted glasses!"

Painter's palette

In Verrocchio's workshop, young Leonardo learned to make paints, glazes, and varnishes. He used natural colors made from berries, roots, crushed rock, and even insects that were dried and ground into powder. This powder, or pigment, was then mixed with oil to make a paste. The colors Leonardo used are called his "palette"—the same name as the curved wooden board he mixed his paints on.

LEONARDO WAS FAMOUS FOR HIS LANDSCAPES. THE PAINTING BELOW SHOWS THE ORNAMENTAL TREES OF HIS NATIVE FLORENCE.

Colors of nature

Leonardo observed how colors shimmered and danced on water, on a peacock's feathers, and on pieces of glass. Then he imitated the blended colors in his own paintings.

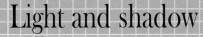

Light and shadow

Leonardo was fascinated by the way sunlight and shadow changed the colors of trees and leaves. This led him to create rules about how to paint accurately. Soon he developed a painting technique called "chiaroscuro" (or "light and dark" in Italian). It gave his paintings the soft, lifelike look that made other people's paintings seem flat and dark by comparison.

13

A Renaissance man

Leonardo da Vinci is often described as the true "**Renaissance** man," because he was interested in everything. He was also good at everything, too. In fact, he was a genius: an accomplished artist, an exceptional architect, and a talented designer. Historians who wrote about him in the 1500s, said he was very intelligent, with an amazing memory. He could easily win any argument.

LEONARDO'S DRAWING *VITRUVIAN MAN*, A FIGURE THAT FITS INTO A CIRCLE AND A SQUARE, SYMBOLIZES PERFECTION AND HARMONY. LEONARDO THOUGHT THAT MAN WAS THE MODEL OF THE WORLD.

Unfinished work

Leonardo may have been a genius, but he failed to finish much of what he started. Some people believe he was a perfectionist who was never satisfied with his work. But it's more likely that he was easily bored, or he had too many ideas in his head and couldn't wait to move on to the next thing.

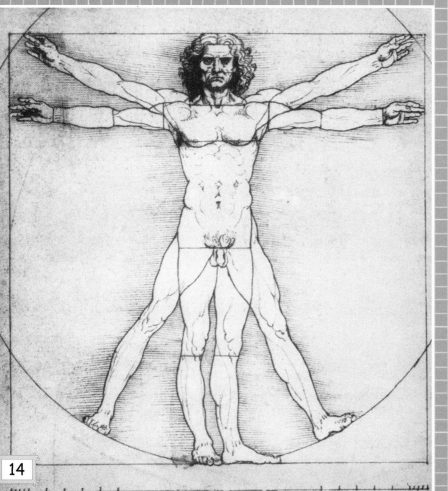

LADY WITH AN ERMINE SHOWS A TEENAGE BEAUTY IN ONE OF LEONARDO'S FAVORITE POSES.

"Leonardo was a real Renaissance man," said Mr. Rummage.

"A what?" interrupted Digby.

"Ah, the Renaissance...now that would have been a fantastic time to be alive," said Youssef," as he strolled up to Mr. Rummage's stall.

"Hi, Youssef," greeted Hannah, "I didn't see you there. You're back from your travels!"

"Yes, I am," said Youssef. "Hello Digby, and hello to you Mr. Rummage. So we're in the Renaissance today, are we?"

"I think so," said Digby, "or at least we would be if I knew what it was."

Youssef grinned, "Well, it was an incredible period in history, when people were rediscovering the wonders of art and science. It was also a time when Italy was made up of a number of city-states."

"I've heard of Florence before," said Hannah. "Was it one of the city-states?" asked Hannah.

"Along with Milan, Venice, and Rome," said Youssef. "They were the main ones."

"Gosh," said Digby, "Italy must have had a lot of kings and queens."

"You'd think so," replied Youssef, "but the states were ruled in different ways."

"Yes," broke in Mr. Rummage, "but the ruling families were always competing for power, so they were constantly fighting small wars against each other."

"Sounds like going to war was a kind of Renaissance sport," said Digby.

Youssef laughed, "Yes—and it was also considered an art..."

"Which is where Leonardo comes in again," said Mr. Rummage. "His many achievements were a shining example of the spirit of the age."

"So what did Leonardo actually do for a job?" asked Digby.

"He was a genius," said Hannah arrogantly, "he didn't need a job."

"Of course he did," smiled Youssef, "even geniuses have to support themselves. Leonardo went to work for Ludovico Sforza, the Duke of Milan."

"What a funny name—Szzzforzzza…"

"Well, it comes from the Italian word for "force," which suited the forceful Ludovico very well."

"What kind of work did Leonardo do?" asked Hannah.

"He was hired as a designer," said Mr. Rummage. "But he spent a lot of his time playing a lute—much like the one Youssef carries in his bag—and singing for the Milanese court."

"Wow! So he was a pop star as well," giggled Hannah. "Can I try out your lute, Youssef?"

The Last Supper

The mural of the Bible story "The Last Supper" is one of Leonardo's best-known works. It can be seen today in the church of Santa Maria delle Grazie in Milan. Unfortunately, because Leonardo was still experimenting with his technique, the paint began to flake off and 50 years after his death, people could hardly see what he'd painted. It was repainted twice, then French soldiers damaged it and, finally, the monks in the church cut a door through its base! Somehow it survived World War II and its luck began to change. Restorers discovered that much of the original mural remained, and now it's completely repaired.

Ludovico il Moro

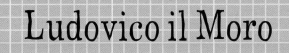

Leonardo went to work for Ludovico Sforza, the wealthiest and most powerful man in Renaissance Italy. Head of the Sforza family and the Duke of Milan, he was nicknamed "il Moro" because of his dark complexion, which made him look Moorish. Ludovico was a crafty politician. He could also be harsh and cruel to anyone who challenged his power. Who would think that a tough man like this could also love fashion and the arts? But he did. And Leonardo had his work cut out for him, in trying to satisfy his master's greed and expensive tastes.

CASTELLO SFORZESCO IN MILAN, LUDOVICO'S STRONGHOLD.

Splendid city

Under Ludovico, Milan was known for its wealth and splendor. Festivals, galas, and pageants were carried out in grand style. Ludovico's marriage to Beatrice d'Este, for example, saw 450 nobles sent to escort her to the city. There were 500 horses in the wedding procession and the whole route was carpeted with the finest white silk cloth.

d'ir. In festo fanctiffimu

17

"Leonardo must have been very bored with all the festivals and parties and stuff he had to go to," said Digby.

"I wouldn't have been bored at all," said Hannah. "I bet it was exciting."

"Leonardo was way too busy to be bored," said Mr. Rummage. "He was designing incredible military machines and proving himself to be a great engineer."

"Sounds as though he was really into war, like everyone else," said Digby.

"No, he wasn't, but it was the only way to get hired by the Sforzas," said Mr. Rummage.

"Leonardo knew the Sforzas were greedy and ambitious, so he made Ludovico a deal. Leonardo offered to show him his secret designs for bridges, battering rams, catapults, and cannons, all of which would strike terror into the hearts of Ludovico's enemies."

"I bet Ludovico really liked that idea," laughed Hannah.

"Exactly! Leonardo was far too clever to see war as a good thing," said Mr. Rummage. "He called it a 'beastly madness,' but he had to make a living."

Leonardo the sculptor

Duke Ludovico was Leonardo's master for 20 years. During this time, Leonardo studied many subjects, including geometry, mechanics, town planning, engineering, and architecture. His architectural studies led him to make plans for entire cities, with canals, bridges, and wide streets, as well as magnificent buildings. Although Leonardo came up with big ideas for Ludovico and his city, few of them resulted in anything.

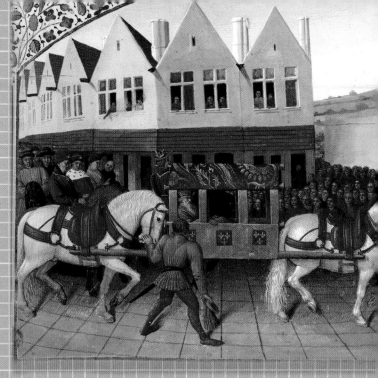

DRAWING FOR A SCULPTURE OF LUDOVICO SFORZA'S FATHER ON HORSEBACK.

Super sculpture

Leonardo could do most things he set out to do, but there was one he just couldn't manage—a huge bronze sculpture of Ludovico Sforza's father on horseback. For 15 years, Leonardo made countless drawings. He also made a fabulous 22-foot (6.7 m) clay model of the *Great Horse*, which the people of Milan marvelled at. But before he could find a way of casting almost 73 tons (66 metric tons) of bronze, the French army invaded Milan. The bronze was used to make cannons instead, and Leonardo had to leave. In the end, French archers used his model for target practice, finally destroying it.

LEONARDO LOVED HORSES AND HE WAS ALWAYS SKETCHING THEM.

Science for art's sake

Although Leonardo enjoyed studying science for its own sake, he could see how to use it to improve his art. Artists, as well as doctors, learned a lot about the human body by dissecting corpses and recording their findings. In fact, during the Renaissance, the work of doctors and artists was very similar—and it changed the way people saw the world around them.

LEONARDO PAINTED MANY BEAUTIFUL PICTURES OF MOTHERS AND CHILDREN.

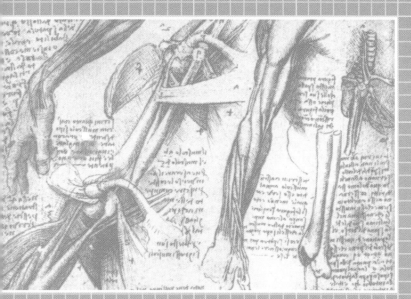

Plaster casts

Leonardo was interested in the shapes inside the human body. He made plaster casts by filling brains, or heart cavities with melted wax. After the wax was set, it was removed from the mold and a plaster cast was built around it.

LEONARDO DREW ORDINARY PEOPLE, TOO. HE WOULD WALK THROUGH THE POOREST AREAS OF MILAN WITH HIS PENCIL AND SKETCHPAD, LOOKING FOR MODELS.

Studies in anatomy

Leonardo made use of his studies of the human body to help him draw remarkably accurate figures. He was the first artist to study the physical proportions of men, women, and children. He used his knowledge to draw the "ideal" human figure.

"Leonardo must have spent a lot of time on his own, studying," said Hannah. "Didn't he get lonely?"

"He wasn't completely alone. He did have an apprentice nicknamed "Salai," meaning "little devil," who he adopted as a son. But he needed a lot of time to himself, especially when he was cutting up dead bodies."

 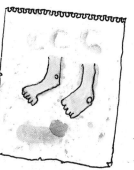

"Oh, gross!" shivered Digby. "What did he want to do that for?"

"Well, he did it because he was studying **anatomy**—the parts of the body. He wanted to know how the body worked and what muscles and bones looked like."

"Couldn't he have used pictures?" asked Hannah. "I mean, getting old bodies and cutting them up just to look at them..."

"There were no pictures, that's the point—Leonardo was the first artist to make really good, lifelike drawings of the human body. Still, it was a grisly job," admitted Mr. Rummage.

"Did he rob graves?" whispered Digby.

"No, he borrowed corpses from the local mortuary. But he had to work quickly so they didn't decay before he'd finished his drawings. However, it wasn't long before the Roman Catholic Church put a stop to it all."

"I can see why," said Hannah, shuddering.

"Did Leonardo stay in Milan with the Duke, Mr. Rummage?" asked Digby.

"No, he went home to Florence."

"Was Florence as much fun as Milan?"

"Oh yes," said Mr. Rummage, "but not always for Leonardo. You see, there was another genius at work there when Leonardo returned. His name was Michelangelo."

"Didn't he paint a famous roof or something?" asked Hannah.

"Well, sort of," smiled Mr. Rummage. "Actually, Michelangelo painted the famous Sistine Chapel in the Vatican City—where the pope lives."

"Huh! And you said "roof," mocked Digby.

"Well, how would I know?" said Hannah.

"Shhh," said Mr. Rummage calmly. "Leonardo and Michelangelo got along about as well as you two are right now. They were always fighting. Michelangelo teased Leonardo for not finishing the bronze horseman in Milan. And Leonardo teased Michelangelo for not coming up with ideas of his own and basing his famous statue of David on classical Roman and Greek sculptures."

"Too may geniuses means trouble," giggled Hannah.

"You're right. And things got a lot worse," continued Mr. Rummage. "Leonardo was upset that he hadn't been chosen to paint the Sistine Chapel."

"Good thing they didn't have to work together," said Digby. "Paint would have flown."

"Actually they did," said Mr. Rummage. "They were both asked to produce a huge mural for the Great Council Hall in the Palazzo Vecchio. Neither finished it, though. Leonardo tried experimenting again and when he left to do something else, the paint ran. And he never went back to it."

Hero artist

When Leonardo returned to Florence in 1499, he was welcomed as a hero of the art world. The work that he had done in the city years earlier had influenced young, up-and-coming artists such as Sandro Botticelli and Piero di Cosimo. Leonardo went on to influence another generation of Florentine artists, including Michelangelo and Raphael.

Michelangelo 1475–1564

Michelangelo i Lodovico Buonarroti Simoni was a painter, sculptor, architect and poet whose genius almost rivaled Leonardo's. Michelangelo was an aristocrat who didn't like being told what to do. At first he just wanted to sculpt, but his powerful and stubborn patron, Pope Julius II, persuaded him to paint the world's greatest fresco on the Sistine Chapel. It was a life's work that took him 29 years to complete.

DAVID IS MICHELANGELO'S MOST FAMOUS SCULPTURE. IT TOOK THREE YEARS TO COMPLETE AND STANDS OVER 13 FEET (4 M) HIGH. DAVID WAS SCULPTED TO REFLECT THE POWER AND DETERMINATION OF FLORENCE. BUT IT PROBABLY ALSO MIRRORS THE SAME QUALITIES IN MICHELANGELO HIMSELF.

"If I'm going to be a great painter," said Digby, "I'll have to study what Leonardo did. So which were his best paintings, Mr. Rummage?"

"Well, it's difficult to say, but perhaps his best known painting is the *Mona Lisa*."

"Hey, I think I've seen it," said Hannah. "Didn't Mona Lisa have funny eyes or something?"

Mr. Rummage laughed. "No, not funny, just mysterious."

"Maybe she was Leonardo's secret girlfriend," suggested Digby.

"I doubt it," said Mr. Rummage, reaching for a large, flat book. "Anyway, look, here's a print of *Mona Lisa*."

"Wow, I see what you mean about the eyes," said Digby as he shifted his position from side-to-side. "They seem to follow me wherever I go."

"What's even stranger is that some people think she wasn't a woman at all, but Leonardo in disguise," said Mr. Rummage.

"What!" exclaimed the children, as they stared at the picture, hypnotized.

"It might have been a self-portrait," continued Mr. Rummage.

"Recent x-rays taken of the painting show a similarity to drawings he did of himself. So it's possible."

"Sound's weird," said Digby, looking confused.

"Oddly enough, it wasn't unheard of in those days for artists to paint themselves into their pictures. Although it's more likely that the *Mona Lisa* is probably a painting of some nobleman's wife."

Famous portrait

Leonardo is well known for his realistic portraits. His most successful was the *Mona Lisa*—short for Madonna (or "my lady") Lisa. The expression on her face is so mysterious, no one who sees it ever forgets it. And her curious smile has made her famous around the world. Leonardo loved the portrait so much he kept it with him, until he finally sold it to King Francis I of France, his friend and patron.

Strange smile

It took four years for Leonardo to paint the *Mona Lisa*. Apparently, to keep her amused, Leonardo hired singers, bell-ringers, and fools to entertain her. Perhaps that's where her smile comes from.

The travels of the *Mona Lisa*

King Francis hung the portrait in his castle in Amboise. But after his death, it was moved from palace to palace. Then, after the French Revolution, Napoleon took it and hung it in his bedroom. When he was banished from France, the painting went to the Louvre Museum in Paris. In 1911, an Italian thief stole the *Mona Lisa* and took it back to Italy. It was found in Florence. After being exhibited around Italy, it was returned to Paris, where an acid attack damaged its lower half. Finally, years of restoration and exhibitions later, it was placed behind bullet-proof glass in the Louvre. The *Mona Lisa* will probably never travel again.

"Did Leonardo stay in Florence to work?" asked Digby.

"No. Over the next 16 years, Leonardo traveled around Italy, visiting Venice, Mantua, and cities in the Romagna region—an area that was governed by the pope."

"Wasn't the pope supposed to be interested in religious things?" asked Hannah indignantly.

"Like looking after the poor and doing good deeds?" added Digby.

"You might think so," laughed Mr. Rummage, "but at that time the pope and many of his churchmen enjoyed the high life."

"Just like nobles," said Digby.

"Exactly," replied Mr. Rummage, "and that was partly because many of the popes came from grand families, such as the Medicis in Florence and the Borgias in Rome."

"Did Leonardo work for any of them?" asked Hannah.

"Well, he worked for Cesare Borgia, who was the son of Pope Alexander VI."

"The son?" exclaimed Hannah, "I thought popes couldn't get married."

"They can't. But in those days, it was accepted that a pope could have children," said Mr. Rummage. "Anyway, it was Cesare Borgia, captain of the pope's army, who hired Leonardo as his military engineer..."

Cesare Borgia

The Borgia family made the papal city of Rome a center of luxury, festivity, and vice. When Roderigo Borgia became Pope Alexander VI, he made his son Cesare, one of his many illegitimate children, head of the church's army. Cesare was a brilliant soldier and a great administrator, but he was also cold, cruel, and merciless. Cesare helped turn Rome into a power as strong as Milan and Florence. Like Ludovico Sforza, the warlike Cesare was mostly attracted to Leonardo because of his engineering skills.

LEONARDO'S ROCKET LAUNCHER, SHOWING MANY GUN BARRELS.

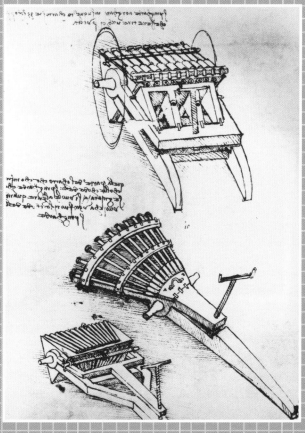

Brilliant inventor

Most of Leonardo's designs were doomed to remain on paper—they were just too ambitious for the times. In recent years, engineers have made working models from them. And although some of Leonardo's inventions don't work perfectly, they still look amazingly modern 400 years later.

SKETCHES OF A WAR CHARIOT WITH REVOLVING BLADES AND AN ARMORED TANK.

Renaissance princes

In Leonardo's day, the "princes" of the city-states were the leaders of very wealthy families. This was the case with the Medici family in Florence, the Este family in Ferrara, and the Viscontis in Milan. The Sforzas of Milan and the Borgias of Rome were different. They were soldiers of fortune—they had fought for their cities and were strong enough to rule them.

The papacy

The popes who ruled in Leonardo's day were ambitious and wanted a papal state at least as grand as Florence or Naples. Rome, with its Vatican City, was the center of the Catholic Church. Here, popes chosen from great families worked to bring order and prosperity to the old city. They also backed artists and writers of the time.

AS WELL AS FUNDING THE ARTS, THE RENAISSANCE PRINCES CREATED MAGNIFICENT PALACES AND HELD SUMPTUOUS COURTS.

Vatican City, Rome

As well as promoting art and science, many popes wanted to turn the lands and cities of the Church into a strong, well-armed state. To do this, they gave their relatives high positions in the cities or cunningly arranged diplomatic marriages for family members. The Renaissance popes made Rome more of a city-state than a center of religion.

ROME ENJOYED ALL THE LUXURY AND SPLENDOR OF A TYPICAL RENAISSANCE COURT.

"It must have been fun living in the Renaissance," said Hannah, "with all those parades and parties and stuff. Do you think Leonardo enjoyed them?"

"I'm sure he did when he was a young man," said Mr. Rummage. "But as he got older he probably spent more time inventing new amusements for them than actually attending them. He was particularly clever at this kind of thing."

"What did he make?" asked Digby.

"Dancing frogs and flying hippos, I'll bet," laughed Hannah.

"You're not far off, Hannah," said Mr. Rummage. "In 1507, he went to work for Louis XIII of France, who was in exile in Italy at the time. Leonardo made him a mechanical lion that crossed the banquet hall, stopped just before it reached Louis and showered him with lilies."

"And it was a great wonder. He was an amazing toy maker, that Leonardo," said Mr. Pollock, who had left his toy stall to join the kids and Mr. Rummage.

Mr. Rummage went on, "Yes, Mr. Pollock he certainly was. But then he was a Renaissance man—he could do just about anything. His sketches show that he made a wolf piloting a boat as a royal wedding present, balloons in the shape of animals, and much more."

"Let me go and get something to show you. Back in a minute" said Mr. Pollock as Mr. Rummage continued.

"Yes, as I was saying, in 1513 Leonardo went to work in Pope Leo X's household in Rome. He set up a workshop and did a lot of projects for Giuliano dei Medici, the pope's brother. He still found time to study more anatomy and physiology, although the pope wouldn't let him cut up dead bodies."

"He must have enjoyed it," said Digby, "working away at being a genius."

"Until Giuliano was murdered," said Mr. Rummage. "That left poor Leonardo on his own."

"Did Leonardo stay in Rome for the rest of his life?" asked Hannah.

"No, unfortunately his bad reputation for never finishing his work began to spread. As time went on, he was asked to do less and less," said Mr. Rummage.

"That's ridiculous," said Hannah. "I'd rather have an unfinished painting of his than anything else."

"Today maybe," said Mr. Rummage, "but although Leonardo was always treated with great respect, he had to compete with artists like Michelangelo, who did finish their work."

"So, did he end up broke?" asked Digby expectantly.

"Oh no, he became the greatest toy maker in the universe," said Mr. Pollock, who'd returned carrying a very strange-looking flying object.

"Mr. Pollock's almost right," said Mr. Rummage. "When it looked as if Leonardo's career might be over, King Francis of France invited him to spend his retirement at his court. He was supposed to be Premier Painter, engineer, and architect, but he spent much of his time making wonderful toys for members of the court."

"Did he make toys like the one you have there, Mr. Pollock?" asked Digby.

"Well," continued Mr. Pollock, "Renaissance people loved balls, ballets, and other amusements. So, Leonardo made fantastic toys for them and ones for himself just like this." And he pointed to the boat with great wings attached to it.

"Wow, a flying boat, said Digby. "Cool!"

"Some people say it's a shame that a great artist like Leonardo ended his life as little more than a glorified toy maker," said Mr. Pollock, as the kids admired his model boat. "But he was always using his imagination, and there was usually science behind what he did."

"That's right," said Mr. Rummage. "So Leonardo ended his days living near the king's royal home in Amboise, filling his notebooks with pictures and ideas. On April 23, 1519, he wrote his will, leaving his possessions to his two pupils. He died on May 2 that year. His last words were, "I have offended God and mankind because my work did not reach the quality it should have.""

Artist's notes

Without Leonardo's notebooks, we wouldn't know how great a scientist, engineer, or architect he was. We'd only know about his paintings. Luckily Leonardo produced 31 notebooks, and even though they were taken apart after his death and scattered far and wide, we can see just how ahead of his time he was and what an amazing imagination he had. Leonardo's notes have been organized into 10 collections, called codexes, which are located in different art institutes in Milan, Madrid, Paris, London, and elsewhere.

AN IMAGINED SCENE OF LEONARDO ON HIS DEATHBED, CRADLED BY HIS FRIEND, FRANCIS I, KING OF FRANCE.

THE NOTEBOOKS COVER AN AMAZING VARIETY OF TOPICS, FROM THE FORMATION OF FOSSILS, AND THE MAKE UP OF THE SUN, MOON, AND STARS, TO THE MYSTERIES OF FLIGHT.

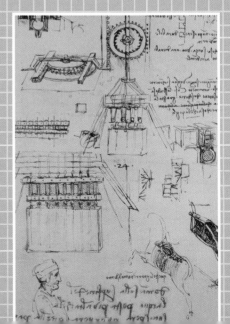

LEONARDO'S GREAT IDEAS WERE SCRATCHED AND SCRAWLED ON FADED PIECES OF PAPER.

"Did Leonardo ever get his book printed?" asked Digby. "I'd love to read it if he did."

"No, he didn't," said Mr. Rummage. "His notes were made for his own use, but they wouldn't have been any good as they were, because he used a kind of backward writing."

"Backward writing!" exclaimed Hannah. "Why would he want to write things backward? I couldn't do it."

"That's because you have a hard enough time writing things frontward," smirked Digby triumphantly.

"Very funny," said Hannah, "but how exactly did he do it, and why?"

"He was left-handed, which helped," explained Mr. Rummage. "You can only read it if you hold the books up in front of a mirror, so we call it mirror writing. As to why he did it, no one knows. Maybe it was to keep his ideas secret, so no one would steal them."

"But anyone could have figured out mirror writing," scoffed Hannah.

"Well, some people say he wrote backward as a way of keeping his sleeve out of the way so he wouldn't smudge what he wrote or drew—who knows."

"Wow, do you think I'll ever be able to get my hands on one?" asked Digby excitedly.

Mr. Rummage laughed. "Not unless you become very wealthy, Digby— at least as rich as billionaire Bill Gates. He bought a collection of Leonardo's notes in 1995—but then he is the richest man in the world."

"Oh," said Hannah. "So that leaves you out, Digby. I can't see you being rich or famous."

"One day I'm going to be a famous painter and inventor, you'll see!" yelled Digby.

"You mean you're going to paint cartoons like Walt Disney?" grinned Mr. Rummage.

"Of course not! I'm going to paint like Leonardo da Vinci, the greatest painter and genius the world's ever seen. And you," he continued, looking at Hannah, "you can be my Mona Lisa. So you'll have to learn to look a little more mysterious."

"I'm already good at that," said Hannah, pouting and staring cross-eyed.

"Come on," said Digby, picking up his palette and putting his artist's beret back on. "I'm going to start right away. Can I borrow the palette for a while, Mr. Rummage?"

"Of course you can, Digby. And don't lose any of your drawings. They may be worth a lot in the future!"

Digby and Hannah waved goodbye to Mr. Rummage and began the short walk home. "I think I'll join an art school in Florence," said Digby.

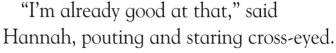

"Is it far away?"
"Oh no," said Hannah,
her eyes lighting up.
"Not far away at all..."

An old man

At the age of 50, while he was living in France,
Leonardo drew a wonderful portrait of himself.
Amazingly, it is the only picture we have of him
that we know is a proper likeness. No one really
knows what Leonardo looked like when he was
young. We can only go by descriptions of him
written by others.

Leonardo: a genius

Leonardo da Vinci was a great artist, architect, and musician. He was a scientist who studied the anatomy of the human body as well as the natural environment. He was also a brilliant inventor who came up with ideas that were well ahead of his time.

In fact, Leonardo could do just about anything he put his mind to. He was a genius. For this reason, he's often given the title of "homo universalis," which means "universal man". During his lifetime, he discovered and created some amazing things.

Here are the highlights:

1482–85 Painted *Lady with an Ermine*, the first modern-age portrait.

1490 Sketched *Vitruvian Man*, one of the most famous drawings ever made. Leonardo's figure of a man that fits into a circle and a square symbolizes perfection and harmony.

1491–1508 Created two versions of *Virgin of the Rocks*.

1495 Began his masterpiece, *The Last Supper*. It took four years to complete.

1506 Finished painting *the Mona Lisa*, a much admired work.

Studied plants, minerals, and the natural environment.

Researched the science of color and developed the techniques of "sfumato" (using transparent glazes to create a misty effect), and "chiaroscuro" (using light and shade).

Drew detailed plans for bridges and war machines, such as the armored car.

Made accurate drawings of the workings of the human body.

Experimented with the idea of flight, designing helicopters and parachutes.

Glossary

anatomy The study of the body structures of plants and animals, including humans

geologist A person who studies the earth

illegitimate Describing a child whose parents are not married

paleontologist A person who studies prehistoric forms of life by looking at plant and animal fossils

palette A curved wooden board, typically with a hole for the thumb, which an artist uses to mix paints on; also the various colors of paints

Renaissance A period from about the 14th through the 16th centuries that is noted for renewed interest or revival of classical art, architecture, literature, and learning

Index

Other characters in the Stories of Great People series.

KENZO the barber has a wig or hairpiece for every occasion, and is always happy to put his scissors to use!

SAFFRON sells pots and pans, herbs, spices, oils, soaps, and dyes from her spice kitchen stall.

PRU is a dreamer and Hannah's best friend. She likes to visit the market with Digby and Hannah, especially when makeup and dressing up is involved.

COLONEL KARBUNCLE sells military uniforms, medals, flags, swords, helmets, cannon balls—all from the trunk of his old jeep.

BUZZ is a street vendor with all the gossip. He sells treats from a tray that's strapped around his neck.

Mrs. BILGE pushes her dustcart around the market, picking up litter. Trouble is, she's always throwing away the objects on Mr. Rummage's stall.

Mr. CLUMPMUGGER has an amazing collection of ancient maps, dusty books, and old newspapers in his rare prints stall.

CHRISSY's vintage clothing stall has all the costumes Digby and Hannah need to act out the characters in Mr. Rummage's stories.

JAKE is Digby's friend. He's got a lively imagination and is always up to mischief.